the KILLERS
DIRECT HITS
2003 - 2013

WISE PUBLICATIONS
PART OF THE MUSIC SALES GROUP
London / New York / Paris / Sydney / Copenhagen / Berlin / Madrid / Hong Kong / Tokyo

Published by
Wise Publications
14-15 Berners Street, London W1T 3LJ, UK.

Exclusive Distributors:
Music Sales Limited
Distribution Centre, Newmarket Road,
Bury St Edmunds, Suffolk IP33 3YB, UK.
Music Sales Pty Limited
Units 3-4, 17 Willfox Street, Condell Park,
NSW 2200, Australia.

Order No. AM1008612
ISBN: 978-1-78305-500-5
This book © Copyright 2014 Wise Publications,
a division of Music Sales Limited.

Unauthorised reproduction of any part
of this publication by any means including
photocopying is an infringement of copyright.

Edited by Jenni Norey.
Music arranged by Derek Jones.
Music processed by Paul Ewers Music Design.

Printed in the EU.

Your Guarantee of Quality

As publishers, we strive to produce every book
to the highest commercial standards.

This book has been carefully designed to minimise awkward
page turns and to make playing from it a real pleasure.

Particular care has been given to specifying acid-free, neutral-sized
paper made from pulps which have not been elemental chlorine bleached.
This pulp is from farmed sustainable forests and was produced
with special regard for the environment.

Throughout, the printing and binding have been planned to ensure
a sturdy, attractive publication which should give years of enjoyment.

If your copy fails to meet our high standards,
please inform us and we will gladly replace it.

www.musicsales.com

MR. BRIGHTSIDE 4
SOMEBODY TOLD ME 10
SMILE LIKE YOU MEAN IT 16
ALL THESE THINGS THAT I'VE DONE 22
WHEN YOU WERE YOUNG 33
READ MY MIND 40
FOR REASONS UNKNOWN 54
HUMAN 47
SPACEMAN 60
A DUSTLAND FAIRYTALE 68
RUNAWAYS 75
MISS ATOMIC BOMB 82
THE WAY IT WAS 91
SHOT AT THE NIGHT 106
JUST ANOTHER GIRL 98

MR. BRIGHTSIDE
Written by Brandon Flowers & Dave Keuning

this? It was on-ly a kiss. It was on-ly a kiss. Now I'm fall-ing a-sleep and she's call-ing a cab while he's hav-ing a smoke and she's tak-ing a drag. Now they're go-ing to bed and my sto-mach is sick. And it's all in my head. But she's touch-ing his chest now. He takes off her

A♭
4fr
G♭
dress now. Let me go.
B♭m7
And
2° 'Cause
I just can't look, it's
A♭(sus4)
G♭
kill - ing me. And tak - ing con -
- trol.

D♭
G♭
B♭m7
Jea - lou - sy, turn - ing saints in - to the sea.
A♭
D♭
G♭
Swim - ing through sick lul - la - bies. Chok - ing on your
B♭m7
A♭(sus4)
A♭
D♭
a - li - bis. But it's just a price I pay.
G♭
B♭m7
A♭
Des - ti - ny is call - ing me. O - pen up my

eager eyes._____ 'Cause I'm Mis - ter Bright - side.

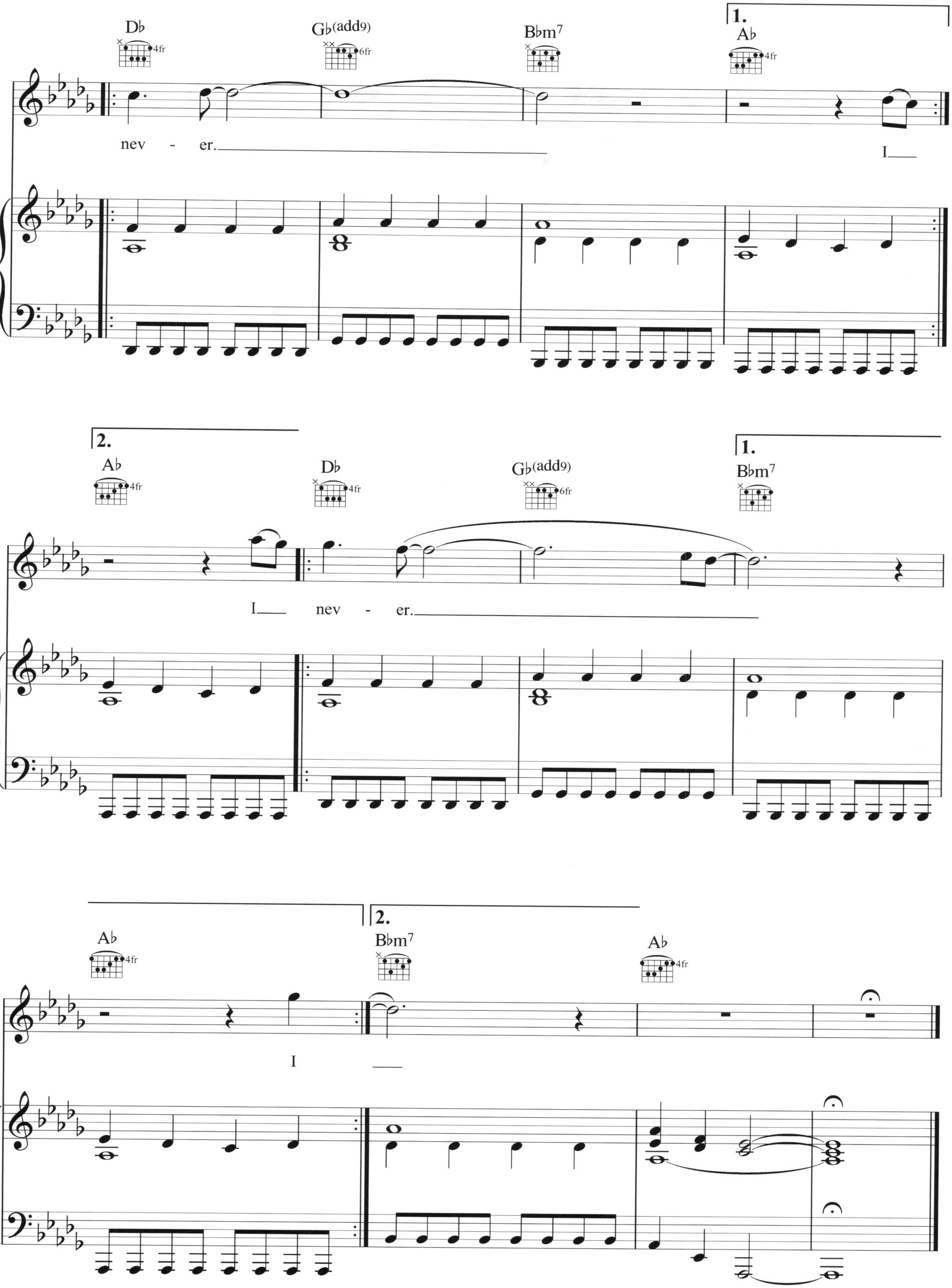
D♭
G♭(add9)
B♭m7
1.
A♭
4fr
6fr
nev - er.
I
2.
A♭
D♭
G♭(add9)
1.
B♭m7
I nev - er.
A♭
2.
B♭m7
A♭
I

SOMEBODY TOLD ME

Written by Brandon Flowers, Mark Stoermer, Dave Keuning
& Ronnie Vannucci

1. Break-ing my back just to know your name. Sev-en-teen tracks, and I've

†Symbols in parentheses represent chord names with respect to capoed guitar.
Symbols above represent actual sounding chords.

© Copyright 2004 Universal Music Publishing Limited.
All Rights Reserved. International Copyright Secured.

E♭m (Dm)
G♭ (F)
had it with this game.
I'm
E♭5 (A5)
break-ing my back just to know your name;
but Heav-en ain't close in a
place like this.
An-y-thing goes, but don't blink, you might miss.
E♭m (Dm)
E♭m7 (Dm7)
G♭ (F)
E♭5 (A5)
'Cause Heav-en ain't close in a

place like this;__ I said-a Heav-en ain't close in a place like this.__

G♭ (F)   A♭ (G)   B♭m (Am)

Bring it back down, bring it back down to-night.__

G♭ (F)

Nev-er thought I'd let a ru-mour ru-in my_

A♭sus4 (Gsus4)   B♭m (Am)

__ moon-light._ Well, some-bod-y told__ me you had a boy-

-friend who looked like a girlfriend that I had in February of last year. It's not confidential. I've got potential.

2. Ready? Let's roll onto something new. Taking it's toll, then I'm leaving without you. 'Cause

Coda
A♭ (G)
F (E)
G♭5 (F5)
- tial, a - rush - ing, a - rush - ing a - round.
Pace your -
A♭5 (G5)
E♭5 (D5)
D♭5 (C5)
- self for me.
I said may - be
E♭5 (D5)
G♭5 (F5)
A♭5 (G5)
B♭5 (A5)
ba - by, please;
but I just don't know now,
A♭5 (G5)
G♭5 (F5)
F5 (E5)
(May - be ba - by)
when all I wan-na do is try.
3fr
5fr

But some-bod-y told me you had a boy-friend who looked like a girl-friend that I had in Feb-ru-a-ry of last year. It's not con-fi-den-tial. I've got po-ten-tial, a-rush-ing, a-rush-ing a-round. Some-bod-y told -ing a-round.

Play 3 times

SMILE LIKE YOU MEAN IT

Written by Brandon Flowers & Mark Stoermer

1. Save some face. You know you've only got one. Change your ways while you're young.
2. Looking back at sunsets on the Eastside, we lost track of the time.

Boy, one day you'll be a man. Oh,
Dreams aren't what they used to be. Some

girl,_____ he'll help you un - der - stand._____
things_____ slide by so care - less - ly._____

Smile like you mean____ it.

Smile like you mean____ it.

And someone is calling my name from the back of the rest-'rant. And someone is playing a game in the house that I grew up in. And someone will drive her around, down the same streets that I did. On the same streets that I did.

Smile like you mean it.

Smile like you mean it.

Oh, no. Oh, no, no, no.
(Vocal echo on repeat)

ALL THESE THINGS THAT I'VE DONE

Written by Brandon Flowers

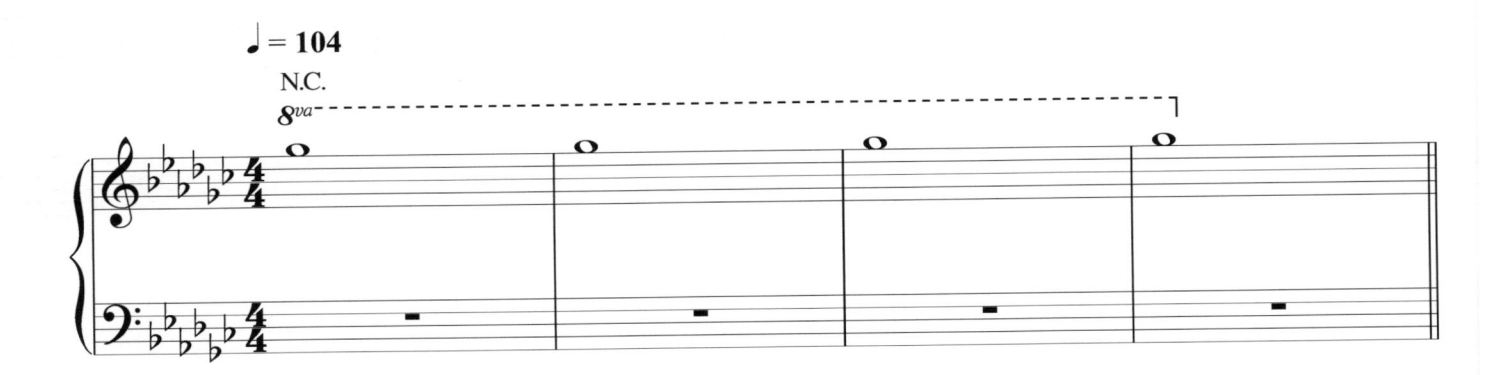

♩ = 104

When there's no-where else to run, is there room for one more song, one more song? If you can hold on, if you can hold on, hold on.

1. I wan-na stand up, I wan-na let go; you know, you know no,
2. An-oth-er head aches, an-oth-er heart breaks. I'm so much old-er

you don't, you don't. I wan-na shine on in the hearts of men.
than I can take. And my af-fec - tion, well it comes and goes.

I want a mean-ing from the back of my bro-ken hand.
I need di-rec-tion to per- -fec-tion, oh no no no. Help me

out,__ yeah;_____ you know you got-ta help me out,__ yeah.____

__ Oh, don't you put me on the back-burn-er._____ You know you got-ta help me

out,__ yeah._____ And when there's no - where_

else to run,__ is there room for_ one more_ song? These chang-

-es ain't chang-ing me: the cold heart-ed boy I used to be. Yeah, you know you got-ta help me out, yeah. Oh, don't you put me on the back-burn-er. You know you got-ta help me out, yeah. You're gon-na bring your-self down. Yeah, _____ you're gon-na bring your-self down. ____ Yeah, ____

____ you're gon-na bring your-self down.

I got soul, but I'm __ not a sol - dier. __

I got soul, but I'm __ not a sol - dier. __ I got soul, but I'm __

27

not a sol - dier. I got soul, but I'm not a sol - dier. I got soul, but I'm not a sol - dier. I got soul, but I'm not a sol - dier. I got soul, but I'm not a sol - dier. I got soul, but I'm not a sol-dier. I got soul, but I'm not a sol-dier.

Yeah, you know you got-ta help me out, yeah.

Oh, don't you put me on the back-burn-er. You know you got-ta help me

G♭
out, yeah. You're gon-na bring your-self down.
(G♭)
Yeah, you're gon-na bring your-self down, yeah.
Oh, don't you put me on the
C♭
back-burn-er. You're gon-na bring your-self down.
G♭
Yeah, you're gon-na bring your-self down.
E♭m
6fr
O-ver and in,

last call for sin. While ev-'ry-one's lost, the bat-tle is won with all these things that I've done. All these things that I've done.

If you can__ hold__ on.__

If you can__ hold on.__

WHEN YOU WERE YOUNG

Written by Brandon Flowers, Mark Stoermer, Dave Keuning
& Ronnie Vannucci

1, 3. You sit there in your heart-ache. Wait-ing on some
2. Can we climb this moun-tain? I don't know. High-er now than ev -

© Copyright 2006 Universal Music Publishing Limited.
All Rights Reserved. International Copyright Secured.

33

beau - ti - ful boy__ to,__ to save you from your__ old ways.
-er be - fore.__ I__ know we can make it if we take it slow.

You play for - give - ness. Watch it now, here he come! He
Let's take it eas - y. Eas - y now, watch it go. We're

[E]
does - n't look a thing like Je - sus__ but he
burn - ing down the high - way sky - line__ on the

[F#] [G#m]

[B]
talks like a gen - tle - man. Like you im - ag - ined when you__
back of a hur - ri - cane that start - ed turn - ing when you__

[E]

34

To Coda
F♯
G♯m
4fr
B
were young.
were young.
1.
E
2.
E
When you were young.
F♯
G♯m
4fr
B
E
And some -
F♯
G♯m
4fr
B
- times you close your eyes and see the place where you used to live

when you___ were young.___

They say the

Dev - il's wa - ter, it ain't so sweet. You don't have to drink right now. But you can dip your feet ev - 'ry once in a lit - tle while.

(Talks like a gen-tle-man. Like you im-ag-ined.) When you were young.

Lyrics:

I said, he doesn't look a thing like Jesus.

He doesn't look a think like Jesus.

But more than you'll ev-er know.

READ MY MIND

Written by Brandon Flowers, Dave Keuning & Mark Stoermer

Driving ♩ = 130

1. On the cor-ner of Main Street, just try'n' to keep it in line,

you say you wan-na move on and you say I'm fall-ing be-hind. Can you read my

© Copyright 2006 Universal Music Publishing Limited.
All Rights Reserved. International Copyright Secured.

mind?

Can you read my

mind?

2. I nev-er real-ly gave up on break-in' out of this
3. It's fun-ny how you just break on down, wait-ing on some

two-star town, I got the green light, I got in a lit-tle fight,
sign. I pull up to the front of your drive-way

I'm gon-na turn this thing a-round. Can you read my mind?
with mag-ic soak-ing my spine. Can you read my mind?

Can you read my
Can you read my

mind? The good old days,
mind? The teen-age queen,

the ho-nest man, the rest-less heart, the prom-ised land. A sub-tle kiss
the load-ed gun, the drop-dead dream, the cho-sen one. A south-ern drawl,

— that no one sees, a bro-ken wrist and a big tra-peze.
— and a world un-seen, a cit-y wall and a tram-po-line.

Oh well, I don't mind, you don't mind, 'cause I don't
Oh well, I don't mind you don't mind, 'cause I don't

shine if you don't shine. Be-fore you go, can you read my
shine if you don't shine. Be-fore you jump, tell me what you

mind?
find.

Can you read my mind?

Slip-ping in my faith__ un-til I fall,__ he nev-er re-turned__ that call.__ Wom-an, o-pen the door,__

[Gb] — don't let it sting,___ [Db] I wan-na breathe that [Ab] fire a-gain.

[Absus4] She said, I don't mind,___ if [Bbm] you don't mind___ [Ab] 'cause I don't shine

[Gb] ___ if you don't shine.___ [Db] Put your back on me, [Db/C] ah, put your back on [Bbm] me,___

[Ab] ___ ah, put your back on___ me. [Gb]

The stars are blaz-ing like re-bel dia-monds, cut out of the sun

Can you read my mind?

Ah.

HUMAN

Written by The Killers

| Gm | E♭ | F |

-der   I was brought but   I was kind._____   And
-mance,   they al-ways did the   best they could._____   And

| B♭ | Dm | E♭ |

some-times I get ner-vous   when I see an o-pen door.
so long   to de-vo-tion,   you taught me ev-'ry-thing I know.

| Gm | E♭ |

Close your eyes,_____ clear your heart,_____
Wave good-bye,_____ wish me well._____

| F | B♭ |

cut the cord._____
You've got-ta let me go.   Are we hu-

48

-man or are we dan-cer? My sign is vi-tal, my hands are cold. And I'm on my knees looking for the an-swer. Are we hu-man or are we dan-cer?

Lyrics:

2. Pay my re-

Will your sys-tem be al-right when you dream of home to-night.

There is no mes-sage we're re-ceiv-ing. Let me know, is your heart still beat-ing? Are we hu-man or are we dan-cer? My sign is vi-tal, my hands are cold. And I'm on my knees looking for the an-swer. You've got-ta let me know

Are we hu-man or are we dan-cer?

My sign is vi-tal, my hands are cold. And I'm

on my knees looking for the an-swer. Are we

hu-man or are we danc-er?

Are we hu-man_ or are we dan-cer?_ Are we hu-man_ or are we dan-cer?_

Instrumental ad lib.

Repeat and fade

FOR REASONS UNKNOWN

Written by Brandon Flowers

E♭5
6fr
B♭5
6fr
clos - er,
I move a lit-tle bit
clos - er.
For
A♭5
4fr
A♭5
4fr
rea - sons un - known.
I caught my stride,
(2.) sat down in
I
the
flew and flied.
o - pen chair.
I know if des - ti - ny's kind,
I said if des - ti - ny's kind,
I've got the rest
I've got the rest
E♭5
6fr
B♭5
6fr
Bdim
6fr
C5
3fr
on my mind.
on my mind.
But my heart
it don't beat,
it don't beat

[A♭5] the way it used to. And my eyes, [E♭5] they don't see you no more.

[B♭5] [Bdim] And my lips, [C5] they don't kiss, they don't kiss

[A♭5] the way they used to. [E♭5] { And my eyes don't rec-og-nise you no more.
{ And my eyes don't rec-og-nise you at all.

[B♭5] [Bdim] [E♭5] For rea-sons un-known. [F5]

For rea - sons un - known.

2. There was an o - pen chair. We

See my heart it don't beat, it don't beat the way it used

57

B♭5 E♭5 F5 C5
6fr 6fr 3fr
to. And my eyes don't rec-og - nise you no more.
B♭5 Bdim C5 A♭5 E♭5
6fr 6fr 3fr 4fr 6fr
And my lips, they don't kiss, they don't kiss the way they used
B♭5 Bdim C5 A♭5 E♭5
6fr 6fr 3fr 4fr 6fr
to. And my eyes don't rec-og - nise you no more.

For rea - sons un - known.

For rea - sons un - known.

For

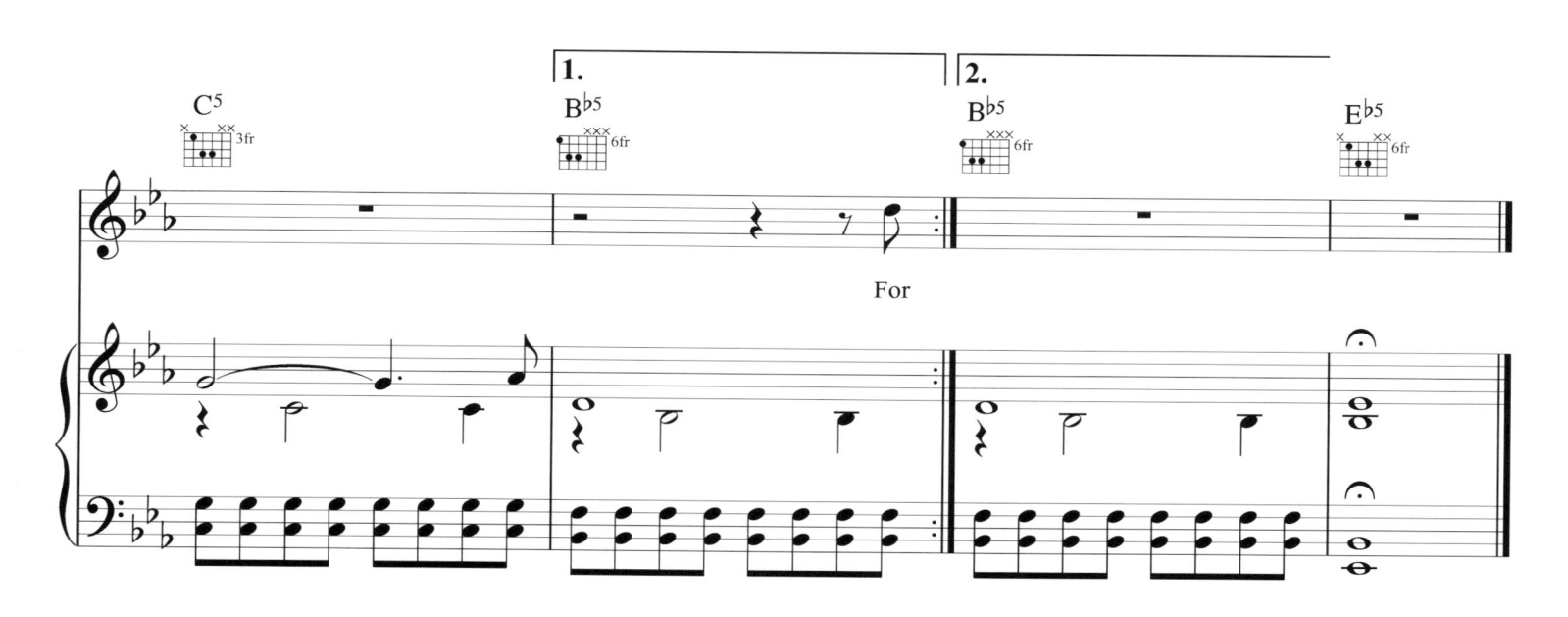

59

SPACEMAN

Written by The Killers

1. It started with a low light. Next thing I knew they ripped me from my bed and then they took my blood-type. It left a strange impression in my head. You know that I was hoping that I could leave this star-crossed world behind,

2. Well, now I'm back at home and I'm looking forward to this life I live. You know it's gonna harm me, so hesitation to this life I give. You think you might cross over, you're caught between the devil and the deep blue sea.

___ but when they cut me o - pen I guess I changed my mind.___
___ You'd bet-ter look it o - ver. Be-fore you make that leap.___

A B

And you know I___ might___ have just
And you know I'm___ fine,___ but I

C#m G#m A B

flown too___ far___ from the floor this___ time. 'Cause they're
hear those___ voic-es at night. Some-times they

C#m G# A

call-ing me by___ my name.___ And they're zip-ping white light beams,
jus-ti-fy___ my claim.___ And the pub-lic don't dwell on

62

| B | G#/B# | C#m |

dis - re - gard - ing bombs___ and sat - el - lites.
my trans - mis - sion, 'cause it was - n't tel - e - vised.

| B | B7 |

That was the turn - ing point.___ That was one lone - ly night._____
But it was a turn - ing point.___ Oh, what a lone - ly night._____

Drums

| E | C#m | E | A |

The star - mak - er says it ain't so bad. The dream - mak - er's gon - na make you mad.___

| A6 | C#m | G#m | B |

The space - man says ev - 'ry - bod - y look down. It's all in your___ mind.

| E | C#m | E | A |

The star-mak-er says it ain't so bad. The dream-mak-er's gon-na make you mad.

| A6 | C#m | G#m | B |

The space-man says ev-'ry-bod-y look down. It's all in your mind.

N.C.

Effects

N.C.

My glob-al pos-i-tion sys-tems are vo-cal-ly ad-dressed.

Sheet music excerpt with lyrics:

"They say the Nile used to run from east to west.

They say the Nile used to run from east to west.

I'm fine, but I hear those voices at night, some-time."

E
B/D♯
4fr
A
The star - mak-er says it ain't so bad.
The dream - mak-er's gon-na
E/G♯
B
C♯m
4fr
make you mad.
The space - man says ev-'ry-bod-y look down.
1.
2.
A
B
A
B
It's all in your mind.
It's all in your
E
C♯m
4fr
E
Oh oh oh oh oh oh.
Oh oh oh oh
mind.

A A6 C♯m
— oh oh. Oh oh oh — oh — oh oh.
G♯m
Oh oh oh — oh — oh oh.
1. B
It's all in my
2. B
— oh oh.
E C♯m E Aadd9
Oh oh oh — oh — oh oh. Oh oh oh — oh — oh oh.
A C♯ G♯m B
Repeat and fade
Oh oh oh — oh — oh oh. Oh oh oh — oh — oh oh.

A DUSTLAND FAIRYTALE

Written by The Killers

A dust-land fair-y-tale be-gin-ning but just an-oth-er white trash coun-ty kiss. In six-ty-one, long brown hair and fool-ish eyes. He looked just like you'd want him to, some kind-a slick chrome A-me-ri-can prince.

© Copyright 2008 Universal Music Publishing Limited.
All Rights Reserved. International Copyright Secured.

blue jean serenade. Moon River what'd you do to me? I don't believe you. Saw Cinderella in a party dress, but she was looking for a nightgown. I saw the devil wrapping up his hands. He's getting ready for the showdown. I saw the minute that I turned away

[Sheet music]

Bm | A/C# | D

I got my mon-ey on a palm to-night.

♩ = 136
D | D/A

A change came in dis-guise of rev-e-la-tion, set his soul

G | D/A | Bm | Gmaj7

on fire. She says she al-ways knew he'd come a-round.

D

And the dec-ades dis-ap-pear

70

like sinking ships. But we persevere. God gives us hope but we still fear what we don't know. The mind is poison. Castles in the sky sit stranded, vandalised. My drawbridge is closing.

𝄋 D/F♯
Bm
Saw Cin-der-el-la in a par-ty dress___ but she was
𝄋 die. Now Cin-der-el-la don't you go to sleep;___ it's such a
A/C♯
look-ing for a night-gown.___ I saw the dev-il wrap-ping up his hands.___
bit-ter form of re-fuge.___ Oh, don't you know the king-dom's un-der siege___
D
D/F♯
G
___ He's get-ting read-y for the show-down.___ I saw the
___ and ev-'ry-bod-y needs you?___ Is there still
D/F♯
F♯7
Bm
A/C♯
end-ing when they turned the page.___ I took my mon-ey and I ran a-way,___
mag-ic in the mid-night___ sun,___ or did you leave it back in six-ty-one?___

straight to the val - ley of the great di - vide. Out where the dreams are
In the ca - dence of a young man's eyes.

high. Out where the wind don't blow. Out here the good girls

die. And the sky won't snow. Out here the bird don't

sing. Out here the field don't grow.

73

A/C♯
Bm
B7
Out here the bell don't ring.
Out here the bell don't
Em
G
D.S. al Coda
N.C.
ring.
Out here the good girls
Coda
G
A
D
Out where the dreams are high.
1.
2.
D

RUNAWAYS

Song by Flowers
Music by The Killers

1. Blonde hair blowin' in the summer wind. A blue-eyed girl playing in the sand. I'd been on her trail for a little while. But
2. We got engaged on a Friday night. I swore on the head of our unborn child that I could take care of the three of us. But

that was the night that she broke down and held my hand. A teen-age rush,
I got the ten-den-cy to slip when the nights get wild. It's in my blood.

she said, "Ain't we all just run a-ways? We got time,
She said she might just run a-way some-where else,

but that ain't much." We can't wait
some place good.

till to-mor-row. You got-ta

know that this is real, ba-by, why you wan-na fight it? It's the one thing you can choose.

Oh!

1. Let's take a chance, ba-by we can't lose. Ain't we all just

2. run-a-ways? I knew it when I met you, I'm not gon-na

A♭ D♭ A♭ G♭
let you run a - way. I knew it when I
D♭ A♭ Fm
held you, I was - n't let - tin' go. We used to look at the stars and con - fess
B♭m G♭
our dreams. Hold each oth - er till the morn - ing light. We
D♭ B♭m A♭
used to laugh; now we on - ly fight. Ba - by are you lone - some

now? At night I come home after they go to sleep. Like a stumbling ghost, I haunt these halls. There's a picture of us on our wedding day. I recognize the girl but I can't settle in these walls. We can't

wait_____ till to-mor-row.___

No, we're caught up in the ap-peal,__ ba-by, why you wan-na hide it? It's the last thing__ on my mind. (Why you wan-na hide it?) I turn the en-gine o-ver and my bod-y just__ comes__ a-live._____ Ain't we all just run-a-ways? I knew it when I met you, I'm not gon-na let you run a-way. I knew it when I held you, I wasn't lettin' go, oh, oh, oh, oh, oh, oh. (Ain't we all just run-a-ways?) Yeah.

Repeat ad lib.

MISS ATOMIC BOMB

Written by Flowers and Vannucci

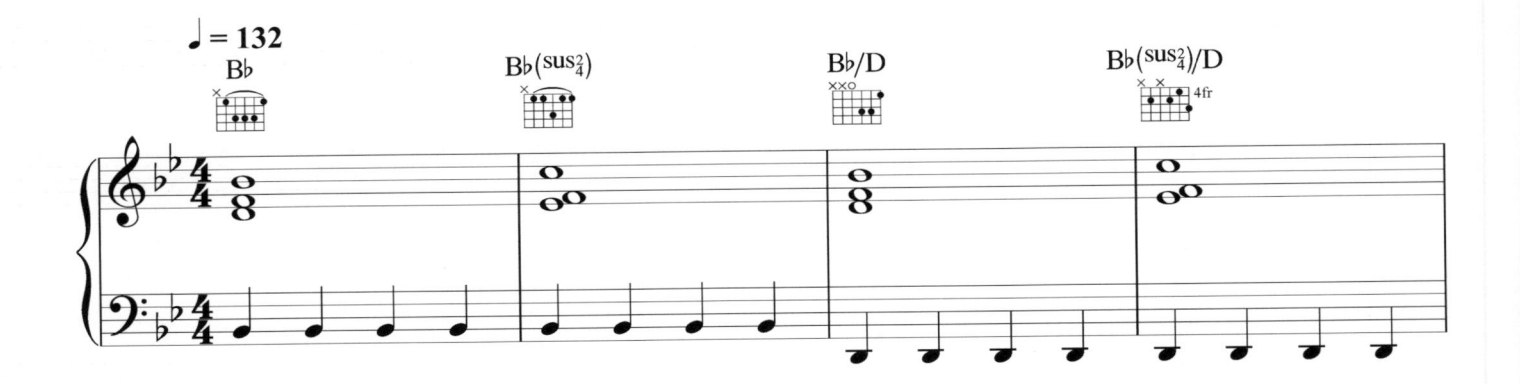

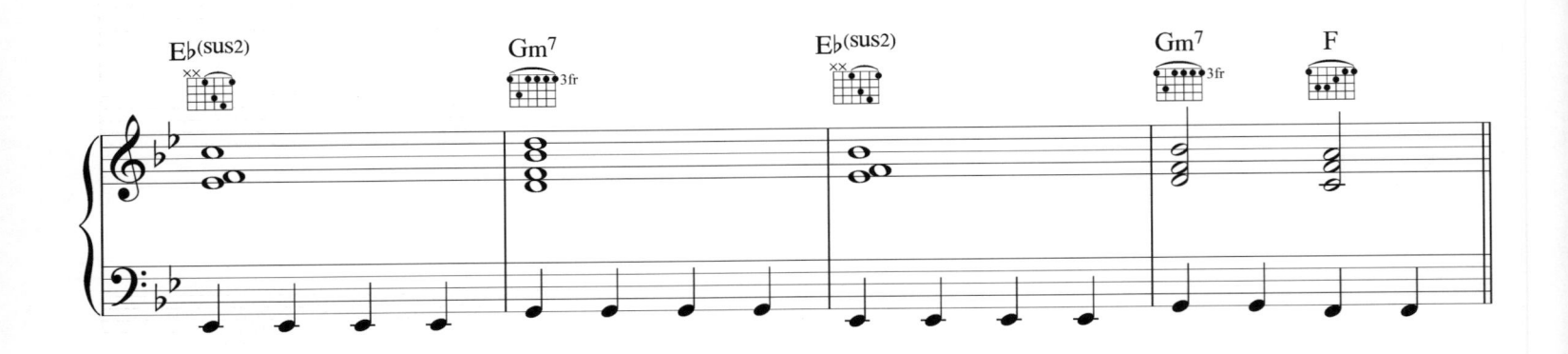

1. You were stand-ing with your girl-friends in the street.

Fall-ing back on for-ev-er, I won-der what you came to be.

I was new in town, the boy with the ea-ger eyes.

I nev-er was a quit-ter, o--bli-vi-ous to school girls' lies.

And when I look back on those ne-on nights, the leather seat, the pass-age rite, I feel the heat, I see the light from Miss A-tom-ic Bomb.

Mak-ing out, we got the ra-di-o on. You're gon-na miss me when I'm gone. You're gon-na miss me when I'm gone. Rac-ing

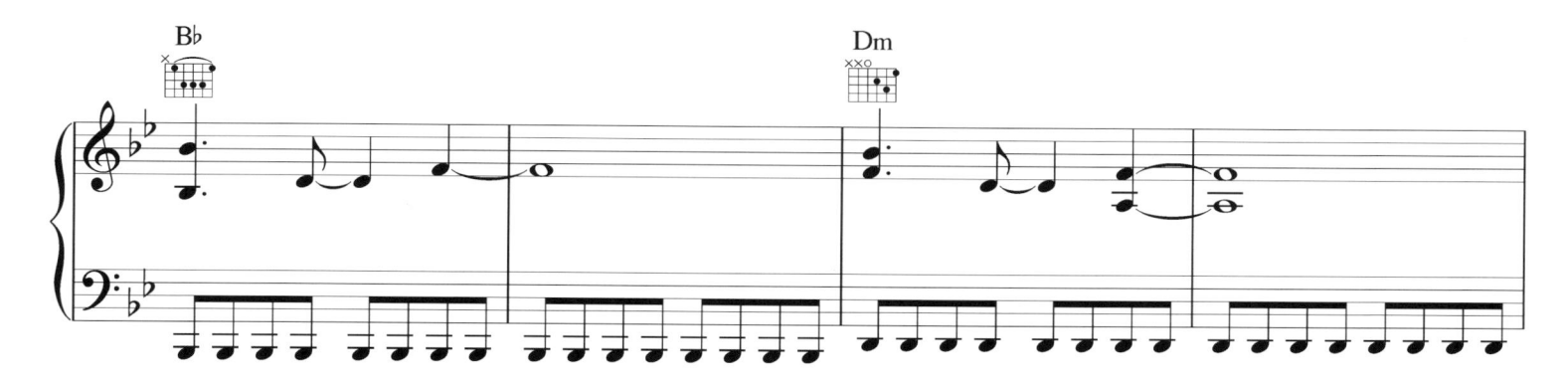

shad-ows in the moon-light, through the des-ert on a hot night.
(%) tak - ing chanc-es on a hot night.
And for a sec-ond there we'd won. Yeah, we were in-no-cent and young.

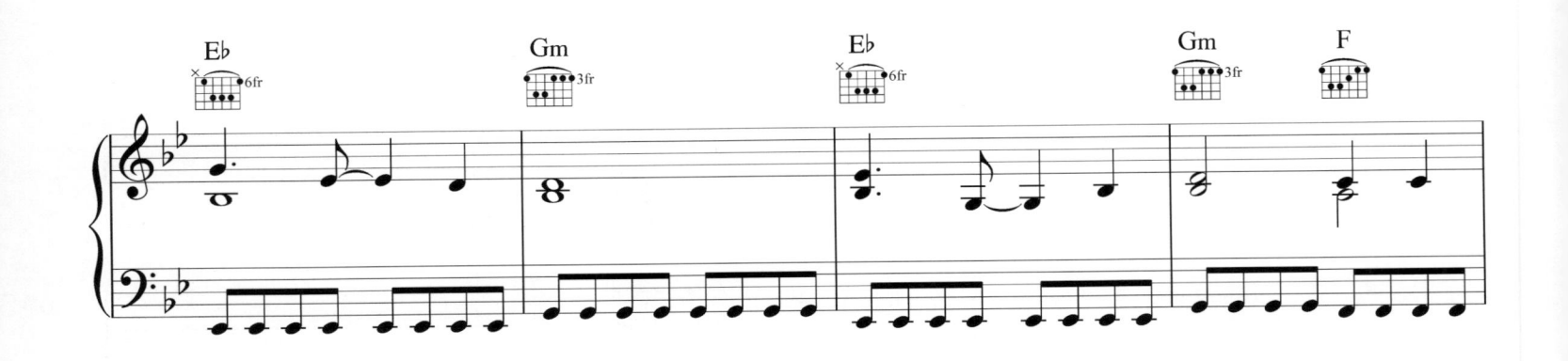

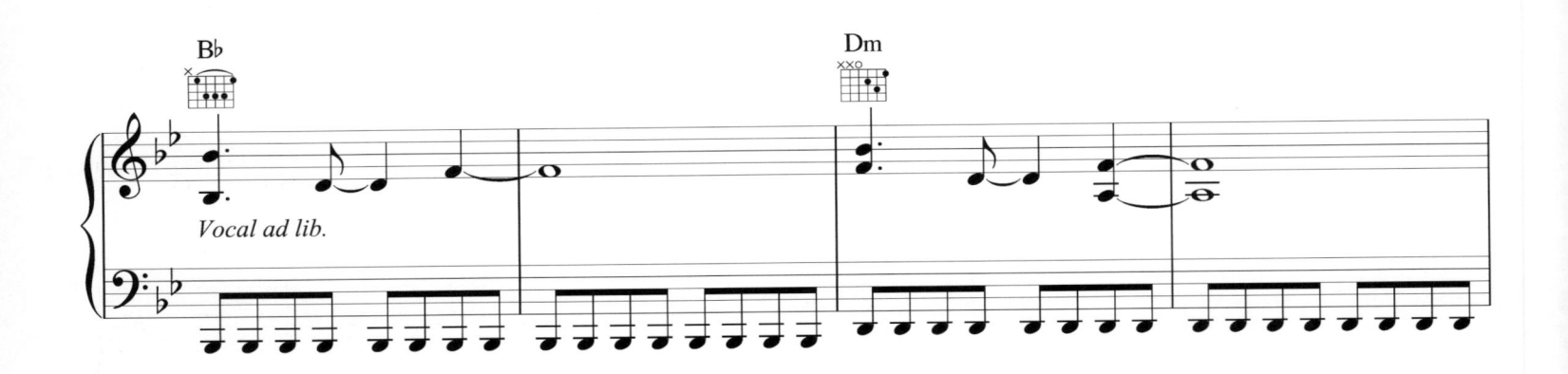

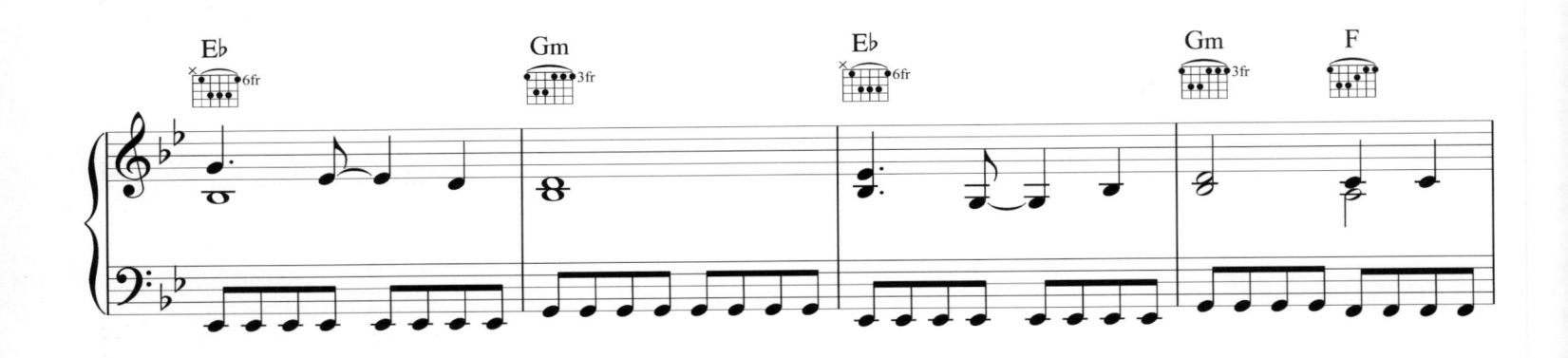

2. Cast out of the night,___ well, you got a fool-ish heart.___

E♭
B♭
So you took your place, but the fall from grace was the hard-
F
E♭
B♭
-est part.
It feels just like a dag-ger bur-ied
Dm
deep in your back. You run for cov-er but you can't es-cape the se-cond at-tack. Your soul was
E♭
B♭
F
in-no-cent, you kissed him and she paint-ed it black. You should-'ve seen your lit-tle face

Eb
6fr
Bb/D
Gm
3fr
F
burn - ing for love, hold - ing on for your life. And
Eb
6fr
F
all that I want - ed was a lit - tle at - ten - tion, a lit - tle
Gm
3fr
Eb
6fr
Gm
3fr
ten - der - ness and truth. I did - n't ask for much, no. Talk a - bout be - ing in the
F
Eb
6fr
F
D.S. al Coda
wrong place at the wrong time for Miss A - tom - ic Bomb.

Coda

Lyrics:
The dust cloud is settled and my eyes are clear. But sometimes in dreams of impact I still hear__ Miss Atomic Bomb.__

I'm standing__ here,__ sweat on my skin.
But I'm standing__ here,__ and you're__ too late.

E♭ Gm E♭
And this love that I've cra - dled is
Your shock - wave whis - pered and
Gm F B♭
wear - ing thin. It's a prov - ing ground
sealed your fate. But you can't sur - vive
Dm E♭
and you took a chance on a
when you want it all. There's an -
Gm E♭ Gm F
Repeat to fade
los - er's game. Miss A - tom - ic Bomb.
-oth - er side.

THE WAY IT WAS

Written by Flowers, Keuning, Stoermer, Vannucci
& Lanois

1. I drove through the desert last night.

© Copyright 2012 Universal Music Publishing Limited & Universal/MCA Music Limited.
All Rights Reserved. International Copyright Secured.

I car-ried the weight of our last fight.

El-vis sing-ing "Don't be cruel" and I won-der if you feel it too, it's like

we're go-ing un-der. Some-where out-side the lone-ly Es-me-rel-da coun-ty

line. The ques-tion of my heart came to my mind. If I go on with

E
A/C♯
E/B
B
you can it be the way it was when we
A
E
B
B(sus4)
met? Did you for - get all a - bout those gold - en nights?
3
E
C♯m
4fr
G♯m
4fr
2. May - be a thief stole your heart,
A
B
E
B
or may - be we just drift - ed a -

-part.___ I re-mem-ber driv-ing in my dad-dy's car_ to the air-field. Blank-et on the hood, backs_ a-gainst the wind-shield. Back then this thing was run-ning on mo-men-tum, love and trust. That pa-ra-dise is bu-ried in the dust. If I go on with you can it

A/C♯
E/B
B
A
be the way it was when we met? Did you for-
E
B
B(sus4)
-get all a-bout those gold - en nights?
F♯m7
C♯m
All of our plans have fall - en through.
B
F♯m7
Some-times a dream, it don't come
3
4fr

96

1.
B
B(sus4)
2.
B
- en nights?
If I go of.
Can it
E
C#m
be the way it was?
G#m
A
B
E
May-be a thief
Repeat ad lib. to fade
C#m
G#m
A
B
stole your heart.

JUST ANOTHER GIRL

Written by Brandon Flowers

♩ = 136

Con pedale

Step out in-to the In-di-an dust.

I can feel the cracks in my spi-rit. They're start-ing to bust.

© Copyright 2013 Universal Music Publishing Limited.
All Rights Reserved. International Copyright Secured.

Lyrics:
Drive by your house, nobody's home.
I'm trying to tell myself that I'm better off alone.
All of my friends say I should move on.

D♯m
6fr
She's just an - oth - er girl.
B
C♯
4fr
F♯
3
Don't let her stick it to your heart so hard. And all of my
C♯
4fr
A♯m
friends say it wasn't meant to be.
D♯m
6fr
B
C♯
4fr
To Coda
And it's a great big world. She's just an-oth - er

F♯
C♯
4fr
A♯m
girl.
An-oth - er
D♯m
6fr
B
C♯
4fr
girl.
1. I
F♯
C♯
4fr
went to see a for-tune tell-er, that was a trip.
May-be this con-fu-sion's got me
(2.) Ja-son's get-ting mar-ried in the blink of an eye.
I got an in-vi-ta-tion but I
A♯m
D♯m
6fr
los-ing my grip.
I can't be-lieve you're out there fly-ing with some-bod - y else. Ah.
did-n't re-ply.
Tell your lit - tle broth-er that we put down the gloves.

102

girl.

All of my friends say I should move on.

All of my friends say, all of my friends say,

all of my friends say she's just an-oth-er

girl. And why can't I sleep at night? And why don't the moon look right? The sound's off but the T.V.'s on and it's a great big world. (She's just an-oth-er girl.) Don't let her stick it to your heart, boy. (She's

B
just an - oth - er girl.)
All of my friends say
C♯
4fr
F♯
she's just an-oth - er girl.
C♯
4fr
D♯m7
6fr
An - oth - er girl.
B(add9)
2fr
C♯
4fr
F♯

SHOT AT THE NIGHT

Written by Brandon Flowers

1. Once in a life-time the suf-fer-ing of fools to find our way home, to break in these bones. Once in a life-time. Once in a life-time. Once in a life-time. Oh.

B♭ F Dm C(sus4) B♭ F
Give me a shot at the night. Give me a mo - ment.
Dm C B♭ F Dm C(sus4)
Some kind - a my - ste - ri - ous. Give me a shot at the night.
B♭ F Dm C F
To Coda
Give me a mo - ment. Some kind - a my - ste - ri - ous. Ooh. Ooh.
B♭ F Am
2. Once in a life - time. We're break - ing all
3
3

the rules____ to find that our home

has long been out-grown.____ Throw me a life-line,

'cause hon-ey I____ got noth-ing to lose.____

D.S. al Coda

Once in a life-time. Once in a life-time. Once in a life-time.____ Oh.____

Coda

Bb | F | Dm7 | C(sus4) | Bbmaj7

Give me a shot at the night.

Oh,_____

N.C.

Ooh._____

Ooh._____

I look at___ my re-flec - tion in the mir - ror

un-der-neath the pow-er of the lights.

N.C.
Give me a shot at the night.

Give me a shot at the night.

Give me a shot at the night. I feel like I'm los-ing the fight.

Give me a shot at the night. Some kind of my-ste-ri-ous.

Bb F Dm C Gm9

Give me a shot at the night. Oh.

Bb F Dm C(sus4)

Oh. Give me a shot at the night.

1-3. | 4.
Bb F Dm C Bbmaj9

Give me a mo-ment. Some kind of my-ste-ri-ous.